W9-CTU-921

Shoulder Buddies

Helping Kids with Self-Esteem

Second Edition

Linda L. Lee and Jesse Lee

Illustrated by Tim Huesken

© Linda Lee, 2007

No part of this publication may be reproduced or transmitted in any form or by any means, graphic, electronic or mechanical, including photocopying, recording, scanning, or an information storage and retrieval system without permission in writing from the author/publisher.

THIS BOOK IS NOT INTENDED TO REPLACE THE ADVICE OF OR TREATMENT BY PHYSICIANS, PSYCHOLOGISTS, OR OTHER HEALTH-CARE PROFESSIONALS. IT SHOULD BE CONSIDERED AN ADDITIONAL INFORMATIONAL RESOURCE ONLY. THE AUTHORS AND PUBLISHERS OF THIS BOOK DISCLAIM ALL RESPONSIBILITY FOR ANY LIABILITY, LOSS, RISK, PERSONAL OR OTHERWISE, WHICH MAY BE INCURRED AS A CONSEQUENCE, DIRECTLY OR INDIRECTLY FOR ANY OTHER USE OF RELIANCE ON THIS BOOK. QUESTIONS AND CONCERNS ABOUT MENTAL OR PHYSICAL HEALTH SHOULD ALWAYS BE DISCUSSED WITH A DOCTOR OR OTHER HEALTH-CARE PROVIDER.

Shoulder Buddies: Helping Kids with Self-Esteem, Second Edition
www.lindalee.ca

Copyright 2005
1st Printing 2005 2nd Printing 2007
Co-Published by 4th Floor Press, Inc.
www.4thfloorpress.com

Lee, Linda Louise, 1960- Shoulder buddies : helping kids with self-esteem /
Linda L. Lee and Jesse Lee ; illustrated by Tim Huesken. – 2nd ed.
ISBN 978-0-9738179-2-8

1. Self-esteem – Juvenile literature.
I. Huesken, Tim   II. Lee, Jesse, 1994-   III. Title.
BF723.S3L435 2007   j158.1083'4   C2007-906757-3

Printed in Canada

Dedication

In memory of Kozmo

Acknowledgements

We would like to again thank our family, friends, and colleagues for their continued support and encouragement. We also acknowledge the many adults and children we have since had conversations with regarding the importance of self-esteem from the first edition of "Shoulder Buddies." We are inspired by their stories and encouragement to continue pursuing our goals. We would like to thank all of you for your suggestions, guidance, and discussions on how to make "Shoulder Buddies" even better. We hope you like the new and improved second edition!

About this Book

To parents, teachers and other caregivers...

Parents, teachers and other significant adults in a child's life are the very first "Shoulder Buddy." Children need to feel and believe they are valuable, lovable, and worthwhile individuals. These messages first come from the adults around them. Although these enthusiastic adults can never just simply give self-esteem to the children they care about, they are instrumental in helping to establish healthy self-esteem.

Shoulder Buddies: Helping Kids with Self-Esteem, Second Edition can be used to promote learning and discussions about healthy self-esteem. We have geared the language and content to early elementary aged children. The younger children in this age group may need help to read and understand this book, but it is vitally important that the topic of self-esteem be broached as early as possible. Discussions could include encouraging children to not only think about their self-esteem but to draw pictures of their responses to the questions such as "what might your shoulder buddy look like?" The earlier we can teach about self-esteem and how to enhance healthy self-esteem, the better. Just as we teach children about treating others kindly, we need to teach them how to be kind to themselves and how to feel good about whom they are as individuals.

Shoulder Buddies, Helping Kids with Self-Esteem, Second Edition has been reformatted, based on professional consultations regarding the first edition, to make it easier to read and be understood by kids. Using visual aids and repetition throughout the lessons, **Shoulder Buddies, Helping Kids with Self-Esteem, Second Edition** is much more interactive-allowing the kids to put the skills they are learning to use immediately. Now, each copy of Shoulder Buddies II can be individually personalized to the specific child, allowing them instant reinforcement of their growing, positive self-esteem.

What is self-esteem?

Self-esteem means liking yourself from the inside out.

Self-esteem means liking who you are...

> No matter how you look.

> No matter how well you score on a test.

> No matter how many friends you have.

> No matter how well you play soccer.

Well, you get the idea.

When you have good self-esteem, you feel happy and upbeat. It's like you are riding on a camel, feeling good and still able to stay on, even when the road is bumpy.

What does self-esteem mean to you?

Shoulder Buddies

If you would like to improve your self-esteem, it might help to create your very own Shoulder Buddy.

You can use your imagination to invent this special little friend who rides on your shoulder.

Your Shoulder Buddy can be...

A person

An animal

Or whatever you would like it to be.

Your Shoulder Buddy can be...

Furry or

Fuzzy or

Cuddly...like a soft teddy bear.

What might your Shoulder Buddy look like?

Your Shoulder Buddy

Your Shoulder Buddy is always with you, cheering you on.

Your Shoulder Buddy can help remind you to say good things to yourself, even on a bad day.

Your Shoulder Buddy will remind you that you are special in your own way.

This friend on your shoulder doesn't talk back and doesn't give lectures.

Your Shoulder Buddy will...

Always find something nice to say to you.

Remind you about the things you do well.

Remind you about your good qualities.

Help you discover what you need to do to feel good inside.

What might your Shoulder Buddy say to you?

Imagine your
Shoulder Buddy
saying something
positive to you.

Liking yourself from the inside out

Liking yourself means liking who you are on the inside and not just for the things you are able to do, like getting good grades or skateboarding well.

Things that you like about yourself can be called characteristics.

Think about the characteristics that anyone can have (but not everyone does) like being...

> Thoughtful
>
> Or caring
>
> Or kind

For example, think about the things that you like about your friends. Maybe they are nice to you or perhaps they make you laugh.

Your Shoulder Buddy will help remind you to like yourself from the inside out.

What are the characteristics you like about yourself?

Your Good Characteristics

Good characteristics include things like showing kindness or care towards people and animals.

When you help someone else, you get a good feeling inside.

Your Shoulder Buddy can remind you...

When you did something that made you feel proud.

How good you felt at those times.

When you made someone smile-that can be one of the best times ever!

Any of these reminders can help you feel better if you are feeling blue.

Can you describe a time when you did something that made you feel good inside?

Remember a time when you did something caring or helpful. *How did that make you feel?*

Doing the best you can

When you are learning something new, it can be difficult and frustrating. The first time anyone plays a piece of music or learns a dance routine, they usually make lots of mistakes.

With practice we can improve at things a little bit each time we do them!

However, even after trying our best, sometimes things do not turn out how we had hoped. It might be a mistake at a music recital or a fall during a figure skating competition.

Your Shoulder Buddy can remind you ...

You did the best you could at that time.

Knowing you did your best will help make you feel better about yourself even when things have not turned out the way you hoped.

Can you describe a time when you know you did the best you could (even if it didn't turn out how you hoped)?

Giving it your best

You get a good feeling inside when you know you gave everything you could to something like a class project or you gave your best effort for the team and just had fun.

You were keen about something and worked on it to the best of your ability.

Your Shoulder Buddy can remind you how good it felt when...

You studied and did well on a test.

You practiced and became better at something.

You worked hard on a project.

Can you describe a time or activity when you gave it your best effort (for example, you practiced something and saw improvement)?

Remember a time when you tried your best. How did you feel?

Do you know what you like and don't like?

Self-esteem includes knowing who you are. Part of knowing who you are is discovering what things and activities you like and what you don't like.

Deciding what you like and don't like is not based on what a friend likes or dislikes. It's about your own, unique tastes.

Your Shoulder Buddy can remind you...

It's okay to be different.

You can like swimming and your friend can like hockey.

Your friend might like ballet, while you like to read.

And that's okay.

It doesn't make one right or one wrong.

You can like olives, even when others say 'yuck!'

What are some of your likes and dislikes?

You are unique

Being different and liking different things is part of who you are.

No one is exactly like you, which means you are unique.

Knowing what you like, and feeling good about what you like, is part of liking yourself from the inside out.

Your Shoulder Buddy can remind you ...

Of things that make you unique.

That being different is part of who you are.

It's okay to be who you are.

What is something that makes you unique?

Think about things
that you like
(that others
might not like).

Trusting yourself

Trusting yourself means believing in yourself and paying attention to the feelings you get inside.

If, for example, a friend tells you to break a window and calls you a loser if you don't do it, you trust that feeling inside that tells you it is wrong to break windows.

Your Shoulder Buddy can remind you...

You are not a "loser" if you don't break a window.

That knowing right from wrong is important.

To listen to that feeling inside that's telling you something is wrong.

To make the right decision.

You will be able to tell your friend "no" and walk away feeling good about your decision.

Can you think of a tough decision that you've had to make?

Paying Attention to your Feelings

A person feels all different kinds of feelings. You can be sad, or mad, or glad. It's important to pay attention to the feelings we have and the reasons why we are feeling that way.

Trusting yourself and paying attention to feelings you get inside will help you to make good decisions.

If you get a feeling that tells you not to do something or that something is wrong, you don't do it.

Your Shoulder Buddy can remind you ...

   To listen to your feelings and don't ignore them.

   Trust that feeling and do what you think is best or what you know is right.

   Make good decisions for yourself.

When have you paid attention to your feelings?

Think about a time when you made a good decision for yourself (even though it might have been difficult to do). How did that make you feel?

Having Confidence

It is very important to believe you can do things. This is called having confidence.

Having confidence doesn't mean believing you are better than everyone else. It is a belief from the inside about yourself.

Your Shoulder Buddy can remind you...

Of things that you CAN do.

Not to pay attention only to things you have difficulty with.

To do your best, even if you feel embarrassed or nervous in a situation.

For example, to feel good about putting your hand up in class and giving your best answer (even if it turns out it isn't correct). Having confidence allows you to try and learn, even from your mistakes.

You can do it!

When have you had confidence?

Believe in Yourself

It is important to believe in yourself.

When you believe in yourself, you will have more fun in any activity you choose and maybe do even better at it than you expected.

Even Olympic athletes need more than just skill to do well in their event, they have to believe that they will perform well in their event.

Your Shoulder Buddy can remind you ...

> If you believe you can do something, you are more likely to succeed at it.

Believe it!

Can you think of a time or situation when you believed in yourself?

Think about a time when you felt confident. How did that make you feel?

Nobody's Perfect

Remember that no one is perfect.

Sometimes you will make mistakes and you might wish you had done things differently or better. That's okay.

If you like yourself from the inside out, you will not put yourself down.

Instead, you might think about what you can change for the next time.

Your Shoulder Buddy can help you by asking questions like...

"What could I do differently next time?" or

"What do I need to do now to help get a good feeling inside?"

Are you kind to yourself even when you make a mistake?

It's Okay to Make Mistakes

Remember everyone makes mistakes.

Even the best players make mistakes. And even kids who do well in one area, such as gymnastics, may have difficulties in other areas, like math class.

We can learn from our mistakes. Remember the question "what might I do differently next time?"

For example, your Shoulder Buddy can help remind you...

"Well, maybe I'm not the best player on the team, but I still like to play the game."

Or, "Maybe I'll play something different."

Or, "Maybe I'll try to practice more."

Your Shoulder Buddy can remind you of what you are able to do.

Can you give an example of when you have made a mistake and what you might do differently the next time?

Think about a time you made a mistake. What did you say to yourself? What might you say differently?

Be Kind and Caring to Yourself

Most people can be kind and caring to others. It is just as important to be kind and caring to yourself.

Self-esteem means taking good care of yourself. Taking good care of yourself does not mean you are being selfish.

Your Shoulder Buddy can remind you ...

   To say nice things to yourself.

   To do nice things for yourself.

   That taking good care of yourself means that you like yourself.

Be kind to yourself!

What are ways you have been kind and caring to yourself?

Take Care of Yourself Inside and Out

Healthy self-esteem means taking good care of yourself.

Eating healthy foods and getting exercise are some of the important ways we take care of our bodies.

Listening to our feelings, liking who we are, and being nice to ourselves are some of the important ways we take care of ourselves on the inside.

Your Shoulder Buddy, who is always with you, can help you to be your own inner best friend.

Your Shoulder Buddy can remind you ....

Self-esteem means taking good care of yourself inside and out!

Think about nice things you can say to yourself. What are other healthy self-esteem choices you can make?

When your teacher's kind of gruff
And the test is kind of tough
Instead of feeling cruddy
Remember your Shoulder Buddy.

Even when you're the last one picked
for the team
Don't forget about Self-esteem.

Liking your Self is smart
no matter what
From the inside out.

Also available from Linda L. Lee and Jesse Lee:

From the Inside Out:
A Self-Esteem Book for Kids,
Second Edition (©2006)

Previously Published Works by Linda L. Lee and Jesse Lee:

Shoulder Buddies: Helping Kids with Self-Esteem (©2005)

From the Inside Out: A Self-Esteem Book for Kids,
First Edition (©2005)

For Ordering Information or Comments and Suggestions,
please visit www.lindalee.ca

About the authors – Linda L. Lee and Jesse Lee

Linda is a psychologist in Calgary, Alberta. She specializes in the treatment of depression, anxiety, and self-esteem issues for adults. Linda has co-facilitated self-esteem groups for over sixteen years. Her son, Jesse, is a middle school student and specializes in homework. Together, this dynamic team thought that sharing their discussions and ideas about self-esteem might be helpful for other kids. Jesse and Linda live with Kim (dad), Diego (dog), and Zoe (cat).